The Bee Who Couldn't Fly

Level 9 – Gold

Helpful Hints for Reading at Home

The graphemes (written letters) and phonemes (units of sound) used throughout this series are aligned with Letters and Sounds. This offers a consistent approach to learning whether reading at home or in the classroom.

HERE ARE SOME COMMON WORDS THAT YOUR CHILD MIGHT FIND TRICKY:

water	where	would	know	thought	through	couldn't
laughed	eyes	once	we're	school	can't	our

TOP TIPS FOR HELPING YOUR CHILD TO READ:

- Encourage your child to read aloud as well as silently to themselves.
- Allow your child time to absorb the text and make comments.
- Ask simple questions about the text to assess understanding.
- Encourage your child to clarify the meaning of new vocabulary.

This book focuses on developing independence, fluency and comprehension. It is a gold level 9 book band.

The Bee Who Couldn't Fly

Written by
Mignonne Gunasekara

Illustrated by
Kris Jones

Bernie Bee was really excited. Today was the day that all the young bees were finally old enough to try to fly.

Their nurse, Miss Beedle, had gathered everyone by the entrance to the hive and was letting them out in small groups.

Bernie huddled with her best friends, Billy, Bella and Brenda. The four of them had grown up together, side by side in the hive's nursery. They couldn't believe it was their time to fly already. They were very excited!

Being able to fly meant they could leave the hive for the first time. There was a whole world out there to explore, and they couldn't wait to see it. Before they knew it, their group was next to fly out of the hive.

"Are you ready?" asked Miss Beedle.

"I was born ready!" yelled Billy, and with a hop and a skip he was up in the air.

"Wait for us!" Bella called out after him. She flapped her wings and flew to join Billy.

Brenda wasn't far behind. "I'm really flying!" squealed Brenda. "Come on, Bernie. Let's go!"

Bernie stepped up to take her turn while her friends watched on. She closed her eyes and thought about flapping her wings.

Then Bernie leapt into the air... and fell straight back down to the hive's floor. That wasn't supposed to happen.

Bernie looked up at her friends and their mouths were open in shock.

"Are you all right?" asked Miss Beedle.
"I think so," replied Bernie. "I don't know what went wrong."
"Why don't you try again, Bernie," said Miss Beedle. "It can take a couple of goes to fly sometimes."

Bernie picked herself off the floor.

"OK, Miss Beedle," she said.

Bernie focused all her energy and tried again.
It still wasn't enough to get her into the air.

"I can't do it," said Bernie. She started to get
a bit upset.

Miss Beedle saw this and tried to comfort
Bernie.

"It's OK, Bernie," said Miss Beedle. "Let's take a break and try again in a minute."
Bernie sniffed and walked off to the side to let the rest of the young bees have their turn.

Billy, Bella and Brenda slowly flew back down and walked over to her. They all started to speak at once.

"Are you OK?"
"What happened?"
"What did Miss Beedle say?"
"I don't know!" cried Bernie. "I... I don't think my wings work properly."

"Do you know that for sure?" asked Bella.
"Maybe your third try will be lucky," said Brenda.
"Yeah," said Billy. "Try one more time."
"OK," said Bernie. "I'll try again."
Bernie tried to flap her wings so hard she thought she might burst, but nothing happened.

"Why can't I fly?" whispered Bernie.
She felt like she was letting her friends down.
They could be playing and exploring outside
the hive, but they were stuck with her instead.
"You should all go back to flying," said
Bernie. "You don't have to wait for me."

"Oh, Bernie," said Brenda. "Friends don't leave each other behind."
Bernie started to walk away.
"No, really," she said over her shoulder.
"I'll be OK. Please go and have fun. I'll see you later."
Bernie ran around the corner and slumped against the hive wall.

What kind of a bee was a bee who couldn't fly? How would she play with her friends? What work could she do in the hive when she was older?

Bernie was snapped out of her sad thoughts by some yelling she could hear in the distance.

It was coming from the hive entrance. Bernie made her way back, only to find a massive panic there. Through the crowd, she saw her friends hovering just outside the entrance. Bernie was about to call out to them when she saw the wasps.

They were big. They were ugly. And they were attacking the hive.

Billy, Bella, Brenda and the rest of Bernie's nursery friends were doing their best, but it looked like the wasps were winning. Bernie wished more than ever that she was able to fly. Her friends needed help!

Bernie wondered if anyone had told the mayor about the attack. Mayor Beety would know what to do about the wasps. Bernie turned and ran deep into the hive to tell her about what was happening. She burst into the mayor's office to find her having a cup of honey.

When she saw how worried Bernie looked, Mayor Beety put her cup down. "Mayor Beety," gasped Bernie. "Come quickly! Wasps are attacking the hive!"

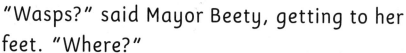

"Wasps?" said Mayor Beety, getting to her feet. "Where?"

"By the entrance!" replied Bernie.

"Those wasps won't hurt any bees on my watch," said Mayor Beety.

She picked up a flower trumpet from her desk. "Attention all fighter bees," Mayor Beety said into the trumpet. "There is a wasp attack at the hive entrance."

Mayor Beety's words echoed loudly around the whole of the hive. There was silence, and then the buzzing started.

All the bees came together to fight the wasps. Bernie watched as bees flew past her, towards danger.

"What's your name, little bee?" asked Mayor Beety.

"Bernadette," answered Bernie. "But everyone calls me Bernie."

"Well, Bernie," said Mayor Beety. "Thank you for telling me about this."

"I want to do something to help," said Bernie.
"But I can't fly."

"Don't worry, you've already helped so much," said Mayor Beety. "And I'm sure it will all be over soon."

Mayor Beety flew towards the wasps, and Bernie followed on foot.

Bernie watched as both the brave fighter bees and the brave ordinary bees battled with the attacking wasps.
Even with all of them working together, the wasps still seemed to be winning. Bernie thought hard to come up with an idea to help. Then she remembered Mayor Beety's cup of honey.

CLICK

"That's it!" said Bernie. "We can use what we do best to defeat the wasps!"

A few moments later, the fighting between the bees and the wasps was stopped... by a blob of honey sailing through the air and smacking a wasp in the face.

Everyone turned to see where the honey had come from.

There stood Bernie, with a catapult made of honeycomb and beeswax. She put more honey onto the catapult and let go. This time, it hit a wasp on the wings.

The wasp struggled to beat its wings with all that honey coating them. It was what Bernie had hoped would happen.

The other bees understood what Bernie was trying to do.
"Quick," yelled Mayor Beety. "Everyone help her!"
Several bees rushed to scoop up honeycomb and beeswax and join Bernie.

They built catapults and started hurling honey at the wasps.

The honey coated the wasps' wings. It was so thick and sticky that the wasps couldn't fly anymore. One by one, they crashed to the ground. All the bees cheered. Bernie and her bright idea had saved the day.

Bernie couldn't fly, but she thought on her feet and came up with the idea that defeated the wasps. She was different to the other bees, but strong in her own way. The hive was very proud of her and Bernie no longer felt like she wasn't a proper bee.

The Bee Who Couldn't Fly

1. How did Billy get up into the air?

2. Where were the wasps attacking the bees?

3. What was Mayor Beety drinking in her office?

4. What was Bernie's catapult made from?

   (a) Sticks and beeswax

   (b) Honeycomb and beeswax

   (c) Sticks and string

5. Why did Bernie feel like she wasn't a proper bee? Have you ever felt that you're not good at something? What did you do?

©2021 **BookLife Publishing Ltd.**
King's Lynn, Norfolk PE30 4LS

ISBN 978-1-83927-399-5

The Bee Who Couldn't Fly
Written by Mignonne Gunasekara
Illustrated by Kris Jones

An Introduction to BookLife Readers...

Our Readers have been specifically created in line with the London Institute of Education's approach to book banding and are phonetically decodable and ordered to support each phase of Letters and Sounds.

Each book has been created to provide the best possible reading and learning experience. Our aim is to share our love of books with children, providing both emerging readers and prolific page-turners with beautiful books that are guaranteed to provoke interest and learning, regardless of ability.

BOOK BAND GRADED using the Institute of Education's approach to levelling.

PHONETICALLY DECODABLE supporting each phase of Letters and Sounds.

EXERCISES AND QUESTIONS to offer reinforcement and to ascertain comprehension.

BEAUTIFULLY ILLUSTRATED to inspire and provoke engagement, providing a variety of styles for the reader to enjoy whilst reading through the series.

AUTHOR INSIGHT:
MIGNONNE GUNASEKARA

Despite being BookLife Publishing's newest recruit, Mignonne Gunasekara has already written fourteen books about everything from starter science and disastrous deaths throughout history to dinosaurs.
Born in Sri Lanka, Mignonne has always been drawn to stories, whether they are told through literature, film or music. After studying Biomedical Science at King's College London, Mignonne completed a short course in screenwriting at the National Centre for Writing in Norwich, during which she explored writing scripts for the different mediums of film, theatre and radio.

This book focuses on developing independence, fluency and comprehension. It is a gold level 9 book band.